Spies & Traitors

© Aladdin Books Ltd 1995

Designed and produced by
Aladdin Books Ltd
28 Percy Street
London W1P 0LD

First published in 1995 in the United States by
Copper Beech Books, an imprint of
The Millbrook Press
2 Old New Milford Road
Brookfield, Connecticut 06804

Design
David West Children's
Book Design
Designer
Flick Killerby
Editor
Jim Pipe
Picture Research
Brooks Krikler Picture Research
Illustrators
McRae Books, Italy

Printed in Belgium

Library of Congress Cataloging-in-Publication Data

Ross, Stewart.
Spies and Traitors / Stewart Ross : illustrated by McRae
Books. p. cm. -- (Fact or fiction)
Includes index.
Summary: Introduces spies and traitors throughout
history, as well as their tools and technology.
ISBN 1-56294-648-X (lib.bdg.)
1-56294-188-7 (pbk.)
1. Spies--Juvenile literature. 2. Treason--Juvenile
Literature. [1. Spies. 2. Treason.] I.Title. II. Series: Ross,
Stewart. Fact or Fiction.
UB270.5.R67 1995   95-13147
355.3'432'09--dc20   CIP   AC

FACT or FICTION:

Spies & Traitors

Written by *Stewart Ross*
Illustrated by *McRae Books, Italy*

COPPER BEECH BOOKS
BROOKFIELD, CONNECTICUT

CONTENTS

INTRODUCTION

Traitor! Since the beginning of history, no word has sent a sharper chill of horror down the spines of those who have heard it.

To betray one's own people has always been the most wicked of crimes, a vile act against Nature itself. For criminals found guilty of traitorous activities, judges, jailers, and torturers have reserved their most cruel punishments.

The most common form of betrayal is spying. When soldiers, rulers, industrialists, and athletes are in rivalry with each other, information about the other side is vital. They will search for it, pay for it, deceive for it – sometimes even kill for it.

This is the sinister world of the spy and secret agent. It is inhabited by men and women of deceit and subterfuge. It has few heroes and little glamour.

Forget the agents of spy thrillers and the glitzy world of James Bond. As you are about to discover, real spying is a nasty business. It is undertaken by devious people. Its background is a sordid mix of greed, shame, untrustworthiness, and fear.

Turn the pages of *Spies and Traitors* and enter this dark world of treachery and intrigue. But before you do – is anyone watching you?

THE DAWN OF TREACHERY

Spying and fighting are among the oldest human activities. Military leaders need information about their enemies, and spies and traitors are always ready to help them. Some seek reward, while others act out of fear or because of their beliefs. There are always a few who spy just for excitement. And with spies come all the codes, tricks, and secret gadgets of their trade.

From the ancient world there is a 1370-B.C. record of the Hittite leader Mursilis sending his chamberlain to spy on Egyptian queen Anches-en-amun, and Moses also used spies in the Bible.

Furthermore, all the great generals of ancient times, from Alexander the Great to Julius Caesar, realized the need for accurate intelligence.

Scalp Secrets
A slave arrived at the house of Greek leader Aristagoras with instructions to cut his hair.

His bare scalp revealed a secret message tattooed by his master, the rebel Histiaeus.

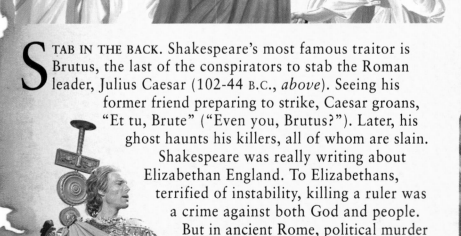

S TAB IN THE BACK. Shakespeare's most famous traitor is Brutus, the last of the conspirators to stab the Roman leader, Julius Caesar (102-44 B.C., *above*). Seeing his former friend preparing to strike, Caesar groans, "Et tu, Brute" ("Even you, Brutus?"). Later, his ghost haunts his killers, all of whom are slain. Shakespeare was really writing about Elizabethan England. To Elizabethans, terrified of instability, killing a ruler was a crime against both God and people. But in ancient Rome, political murder was often thought necessary.

Julius Caesar *(played* left *by Richard Chamberlain) often used spies on campaign. If only he had done the same at home!*

THE SAFE HOUSE OF JERICHO

Before attacking the walled city of Jericho in about 1200 B.C., the Jewish commander Joshua needed information about its defenses.

He sent two spies into the city at dusk, when it would be harder for them to be spotted. Their base was the "safe house" of the prostitute Rahab, conveniently situated near the walls. ("Safe houses" are places available for secret meetings without fear of discovery).

When the King of Jericho sent guards to question Rahab, she let the two spies down the city wall "by a rope through the window (*left*)."

Betrayed by a Kiss (left)
When the Jewish leaders wanted to arrest Jesus, they turned to Judas Iscariot to show them where he was.

Despite universal hatred for this biblical character, ancient and medieval warriors changed sides all the time, and often got away with it!

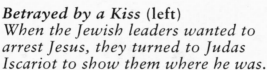

S UN TZU. This 4th-century B.C. Chinese writer (*right*) wrote the world's first military handbook. "Those knowing their enemy as well as themselves," he advised, "will never suffer defeat."

NEWS AS MIGHTY AS ELEPHANTS

The Carthaginian general Hannibal, famous for his battle elephants, almost defeated the Romans in the Second Punic War of 218-201 B.C.

Years before the attack on Italy, he sent spies into Gaul (now France) to find out the best route for the march over the Alps (*left*), and to gain allies among the local tribes.

MEDIEVAL INTRIGUE

Sieges, not battles, were great medieval military operations. With attackers and defenders desperate for good information, siege warfare meant spies and, all too often, traitors.

Under the leadership of Prince Edward, the English besieged the mighty castle of Kildrummy in the Scottish highlands in September 1306. Despite a ferocious bombardment, Kildrummy held firm. Osbourne, the castle's greedy blacksmith, was offered all the gold he could carry if he betrayed the castle. He set fire to the grain stores, and Kildrummy was engulfed in flames (*right*). The defenseless garrison surrendered and was led away to execution. Osbourne stepped forward to receive his reward – but instead of money, he received molten metal poured down his throat (the reward for treachery)!

Betrayed by its own Master
Safe in their mighty castles, the Albigensian heretics of southern France defied the Catholic Church for years.

Queribus (above) fell only when its commander, Chabert de Barbera, was captured and surrendered Queribus castle in return for his release.

THE CRUSADES
The Crusades (1096-1272 A.D.) were a series of eight wars launched by Christian rulers to reconquer the Holy Land from the Muslims. The fighting was marked by great blood-thirstiness on both sides. There was plenty of espionage and treachery, too.

In the First Crusade (1096-1099), pigeons carried secret messages from Godfrey of Bouillon to the emir of Azaz. In 1098, Christians relied on traitorous Firouz the breastplate-maker to conquer the seemingly impregnable fortress of Antioch (*above*).

Norman Soldiers
of the first and most successful Crusade (1095-1099).

They fought in chain mail (flexible armor of interlinked metal rings).

THE POET-AGENT. Sharp-witted civil servant Geoffrey Chaucer (*right*), author of the famous *Canterbury Tales*, was also a soldier, ambassador, and secret agent! His boss was John of Gaunt, one of the most powerful men in England and Chaucer's brother-in-law.

Twice Chaucer went to Flanders on secret business, and his coded messages still survive (*below right*).

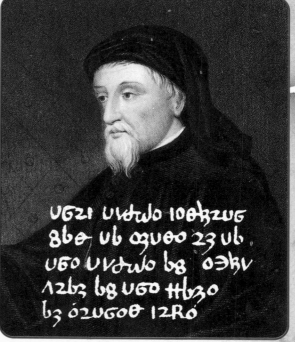

A Tough Nut to Crack
Edward I of England prided himself on having the latest siege machinery, capable of battering most castles into submission.

But Edward was also a master builder, and he had fortified Kildrummy when it was under English control. If only he had known it would be held against him!

Storytelling Spies
Troubadours (below) provided a form of early intelligence gathering. They first appeared in about the 11th century, and were traveling entertainers skilled in singing songs and telling epic stories.

A welcome entertainment in most castles, they could provide valuable inside information about rivals.

SINGER WITH A MISSION
Perhaps the best-known troubadour was Blondel le Nesle. His master, the English king Richard the Lionheart, had been captured and imprisoned.

The legend tells how Blondel traveled around Germany, singing one of the songs Richard had composed. One day, singing outside the castle of Duke Leopold of Austria, he heard Richard singing the next verse in reply from his cell. Now that he was found, Richard could be ransomed and freed.

EAST AND WEST

Mongol leader Genghis Khan was the medieval master of espionage and intelligence. From 1206-1223 A.D. he conquered a vast empire stretching from China to Turkey. He sent spies disguised as merchants and traders ahead of his forces so that when he moved into new territory he knew the terrain and what opposition to expect.

Compared with the Mongols, intelligence in medieval Europe was poorly organized. King Charles the Wise of France used a network of spies to help him keep the peace, and in 1434, England's Cardinal Beaufort set up a system of informers called "King's Espials," who reported on any anti-royal propaganda.

More devious was the "universal spider," the future Louis XI of France. His principal spy at his father's court was Antoinette de Mangnelais, the king's own mistress!

Bronze paizas

GENGHIS AND THE *YAM*

Genghis Khan was the greatest conqueror the world has ever seen. He was a fine administrator, too. He had spies who gathered information, and set up a system of couriers to ensure that intelligence reports reached him as quickly as possible.

Known as the *yam*, it was reported to the West by Marco Polo, who traveled to China in the late 13th century (*above*). Changing mounts every 25 miles, a single *yam* rider could cover 150 miles a day. For identification, couriers carried bronze discs called *paizas*, about 20 inches long (*right*).

Genghis Khan (left) *recognized the value to his enemies of information about his own position. Anyone suspected of spying was immediately executed without trial!*

SHAKESPEARE'S SPIES. If his plays are anything to go by, William Shakespeare had loathed spies and underhanded information gathering.

The tyrant King Macbeth, confessed that he kept spies in the households of all his nobles:

There's not a one of them but in his house. I keep a servant fee'd.

While the interfering old Polonius thinks he is spying on Prince Hamlet (played *left* by Mel Gibson) from behind a curtain in the bedroom of the prince's mother, Hamlet stabs him to death through the curtain.

ANONYMOUS INFORMERS

In 1232, Pope Gregory IX set up the Inquisition, manned largely by Dominican friars, to break the French heresy known as *Albigensianism* (see page 8).

When the Inquisition reached a district, "heretics" had one month to denounce their beliefs. At the same time, secret informers could suggest the names of suspected heretics. When the month was up, (*left*) secret trials and tortures began.

THE INVISIBLE ONES

The Japanese *Ninja* (their symbol is *left*), "those who practice the art of invisibility," were among the finest spies of all time. They were an elite band of warriors, (*right*) at the height of their power in the medieval period.

As good soldiers, they began all operations with intelligence gathering. They were trained to slow their heartbeats, stay awake for days, scale walls, and make themselves virtually invisible against any background!

SECRET WORDS

As soon as people learned to write, they wanted to keep others from reading what they had written. The ancient Egyptians, Greeks, and Romans all devised means of disguising written information. An 11th-century Chinese manual describes how pre-arranged messages could be sent by using the beginning of a line of poetry! By the 16th-century it was common for European diplomats to communicate all sensitive information in code, and many of them employed a full-time "cipher secretary."

The invention of radio demanded new cipher skills – or good luck. During World War I, a German radio broadcast was thought to be just a test signal, until a recording was played slowly on a phonograph and it was found to contain a secret message!

Today, the invention of the computer has taken codes into a world that writers of Egyptian hieroglyphs could not even have dreamed of.

Silky Codes
In World War II, codes for sending messages back from occupied France were printed on silk that could be folded tightly for concealment (top).

CODES AND CIPHERS
The earliest device for encoding a message (cryptography) was a wooden staff. The sender wrote a message on a strip of material wound in a spiral around the staff (*left*).

When unwound, the writing made no sense. But the recipient read it by simply wrapping it around a similar staff of his own.

Secrets on the Wing
However subtle, an intercepted message written in code is likely to arouse suspicion. To avoid this, some agents use carrier pigeons to relay vital information (right) – *a practice that has continued for thousands of years.*

SAMUEL PEPYS' DIARY

Between 1660 and 1669, Samuel Pepys (*left*) kept the most famous diary in the English language. During his lifetime, England was alive with scares and rumors of plot, rebellion, and invasion by the Dutch. In such an atmosphere, it is easy to see why he wanted to write in code rather than in a normal script.

As a result, Pepys wrote in a shorthand that was not deciphered for another 150 years. His diary was finally read for the first time in 1825.

The Enigma

In the 1930s, German scientists developed a brilliant coding device called Enigma. Unknown to them, in 1939 British agents gained access to the secrets. Copies of Enigma (below) were made to speed up the decoding.

A Body of Evidence

During World War I, Russian sailors discovered the drowned body of a German navy officer (left). Death had made the corpse rigid, and in its stiff arms were clasped two books. One book contained one of the main codes used by the Germans to send radio messages. The other had detailed maps of the entire North Sea. The books were sent to the British Navy, and for the rest of the war, they were able to decode virtually every German wireless message.

MORSE'S DOTS AND DASHES

American Samuel F.B. Morse invented the telegraph, the first means of sending a message down an electric wire. But to make use of his invention, he also had to devise a simple means of transmitting language. The result was the Morse Code, which translated the letters of the alphabet into dots (•) and dashes (—).

INTERNATIONAL MORSE CODE

A	• —	J	• — — —	S	• • •
B	— • • •	K	— • —	T	—
C	— • — •	L	• — • •	U	• • —
D	— • •	M	— —	V	• • • —
E	•	N	— •	W	• — —
F	• • — •	O	— — —	X	— • • —
G	— — •	P	• — — •	Y	— • — —
H	• • • •	Q	— — • —	Z	— — • •
I	• •	R	• — •		

The best-known message is the call for help: • • • / — — — / • • •   Can you work out this spy warning? • — — / • — / • • • / — • — • / • — • • / • • / — • • / • • • / / • — • — / • — / — • — • / • — / • • / — / • • / — • — • / • // • • / • • • / / • — • — • / • • — / • / • • / • • • / / • — — • / • — / • • • / • • • / • — / — • • / • — • •

QUEENS OF DECEPTION

Codes, plots, and agents are all part of the tragic story of Queen Elizabeth I of England and Mary Queen of Scots. As a Protestant and a woman, Elizabeth sat uneasily on the throne of England. Her Roman Catholic cousin, Mary, was even less secure on the Scottish throne, and in 1567 she fled south to England.

Since many Catholics believed that Mary, not Elizabeth, should be queen of England, Elizabeth was in a difficult position. The situation was resolved by Sir Francis Walsingham and by Mary herself, who plotted continually for the English crown.

Walsingham foiled several pro-Mary Catholic plots. He also monitored the messages Mary smuggled to her supporters in the hollowed-out corks of beer barrels. In the end, Walsingham built up such a tremendous amount of evidence against Mary that Elizabeth had little option but to agree to her execution in 1587.

A GENUINE FEAR?

Elizabethan England was terrified by the threat of invasion. In 1588, only bad weather defeated the Armada of Spanish King Philip II of Spain (*top*). But the atmosphere of fear also led to many innocent people being hunted down by Walsingham, just as Hoover hunted down alleged Communists in the United States during the Cold War (page 34).

Between 1585 and 1603, 125 Roman Catholic priests were executed for treason. They had been sent to Protestant England to re-convert the people to the Roman Church. Most took refuge in the houses of Catholic gentry, where they hid in secret "priest holes"(*right*).

THE CHEVALIER D'EON

The French spy Charles d'Eon de Beaumont (*right*) liked wearing female disguises. He was so successful with disguising himself as "Lia de Beaumont" at the Russian court of Tsarina Elizabeth that she appointed him a maid of honor!

Later, Louis XV's jealous mistress forced "Madame de Beaumont" (*left*) to flee to England. When he died, a medical examination finally confirmed his masculinity.

Hide and Seek
Priest holes took many different forms. Some were straightforward trap doors (below), others were cleverly constructed using false ceilings and fireplaces.

S PYING – A DANGEROUS BUSINESS. Not only do agents risk torture and death if they are caught, but they can also become a liability to their masters. This was the fate of the young English poet and playwright Christopher Marlowe.

Marlowe was sent to France by Sir Francis Walsingham (*left*) to uncover Catholic plans to assassinate Elizabeth I. Marlowe did as he was ordered. Six years later he was dead, supposedly stabbed to death in a tavern brawl. It has been suggested that he was "removed" by Walsingham because he had outlived his usefulness as an agent.

THE TERRIBLE OPRICHNINA

Ivan IV of Russia, known as "Ivan the Terrible" (*right*), established his country's first network of spies, the *Oprichnina*.

From 1553 onward Ivan's reign deteriorated into a bloodbath. He was convinced that assassins awaited him behind every corner, so he employed 6,000 black-robed oprichniki to destroy them.

They rode black horses with saddles marked with a dog's head and broom, symbols of their mission to sniff out treason and sweep it away. No one was safe from the oprichniki's cruelty. In 1570, suspecting the citizens of Novgorod of treachery, the oprichniki murdered almost the entire population. Finally, Ivan lost faith even in his hand-picked bodyguards, and they were disbanded.

The Waning of the Ninja
For almost ten centuries the deadly Ninjas terrified all who crossed them. Finally, in the 16th century, General Hideyoshi Toyotomi (left) determined to exterminate the troublemakers.

Despite severe losses in battle, the Ninja survived. Shogun Ieyasu Tokugawa found taking them into state employment easier than confrontation.

As mere bodyguards their skills waned, and the secrets of the ninjutsu survived only in a few secret societies.

TREASON AND PLOT

James VI of Scotland suggested that when he became King of England he would look favorably upon Roman Catholics. But when he ascended the English throne as James I, the king broke his word. Consequently, a number of Catholic fanatics, led by Robert Catesby, planned a dreadful revenge. They plotted to blow up parliament when the king, his ministers, and both houses were present.

With James out of the way, they hoped to start a Catholic uprising in the Midlands and put either Prince Charles or Princess Elizabeth on the throne. The task of blowing up parliament fell to Guy Fawkes. He filled a cellar beneath parliament with barrels of gunpowder (*right*).

By November 4, 1605, the day before parliament assembled, all was ready. But news of the plot leaked out. Parliament was searched and the gunpowder was found. Fawkes and the other conspirators (*below*) were arrested, tried, and executed as traitors.

Remember, Remember November 5, 1605 was the day the Papists planned to destroy James I. Ever since, it has been celebrated in England with fireworks (top) and bonfires topped by none other than Guy Fawkes!

TAKING SIDES!
George Downing came from a British Puritan family that had settled in America. Returning to England in 1629, he joined Cromwell's New Model Army (*right*).

With Cromwell dead and Charles II on the throne,

Downing switched sides and earned himself a knighthood by hunting down the killers of Charles I!

He then became a spy for Charles II in Holland, at that time locked in a fierce war with England.

THE CARDINAL'S CABINET

From 1624 to 1642, Armand Jean du Plessis, Cardinal Richelieu (*left*), was the most powerful man in France. He did more than any other minister to make the king absolute at home, and France supreme in Europe.

Realizing the value of reliable information, Richelieu set up the "Cabinet Noir" (the Black Cabinet) – a highly efficient secret police organization – to provide intelligence reports on the French nobility and foreign powers.

He paid its members out of his own pocket and they owed their loyalty directly to him, not the king.

Gentle Persuasion

Louise de Querouaille, (right) the lovely mistress of Charles II, was officially lady-in-waiting to Charles' sister. She was also a secret agent, sent by the French king Louis XIV to persuade Charles to ally with France.

Out with it!

In 1654 a French agent reached Marshal Turenne with vital information.

To protect his message, he had wrapped it in lead (right) and swallowed it. But when he reached the French camp, he could not get it out again.

He succeeded, however, when an officer threatened to cut him open!

KIDNAPPED! Robert Louis Stevenson's *Kidnapped* tells of hero David Balfour (*right*) and Alan Breck, a secret agent sent by the exiled House of Stuart to plan their return to the English throne. After many adventures, including being suspected of murder, the pair escape. The tale is typical of the romanticized Victorian vision of the Jacobites (supporters of the Stuarts). The real Jacobites were hopelessly inefficient at intelligence gathering.

SPIES FOR THE REVOLUTIONS

The American and French Revolutions played a vital part in shaping the modern world. Both provided plenty of opportunity for the clandestine operations of spies and traitors.

The most famous double agent was Benjamin Franklin. An experienced politician who had helped to draft the Declaration of Independence, he seemed the ideal person to persuade the French to assist the American rebels. In 1776 he was sent to Paris.

Two years later, a Franco-American alliance was signed. But all the time, Franklin had been helping the British while ambassador in Paris. He turned a blind eye to a stream of top secret military intelligence being passed on to London.

ANDRE'S END

In 1780, an American traitor offered the British a key strategic position for £20,000.

Carrying papers with this information and dressed in civilian clothes, Major John André was stopped by an American patrol (*left*). Losing his nerve, he blurted out his true identity, and then promised 100 gold coins for his freedom. Unimpressed, American authorities hanged him as a spy.

FOREIGN AGENTS

As head of the British intelligence department, Lieutenant Colonel Colquhoun Grant, set up networks of spies called *alcades* for the Duke of Wellington (*top of page*), during his Peninsular campaign.

Alcades were local Spaniards and Portuguese – eager to pass on information that might defeat the hated French invaders.

Hale Fails

Upon entering the British camp disguised as a Dutch teacher, American agent Nathan Hale (below) *seemed so nervous that he was searched. Messages were found in his shoes, and he was hanged.*

THE DREADED FOUCHE

Frenchman Joseph Fouché (*right*) was the most evil of spymasters. Trained as a priest, in 1792 he joined forces with the French Revolution and supported the king's execution, becoming the bloodiest of radicals. By 1799 he joined Napoléon, who made him minister of police. Fouché's agents helped keep Napoléon in power until 1815, when the self-seeking turncoat deserted him. Fouché eventually died in exile, detested.

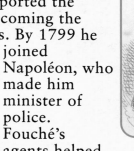

GUILLOTINING THE REVOLUTION!

When both royalists (supporters of the King) and revolutionaries (republicans) were getting caught spying, French Baron Jean de Batz managed to live a charmed double life. He posed as a fervent republican, while secretly running a network of royalist agents.

His favorite tactic was to use the guillotine (*left*), the weapon of the revolution, to destroy the revolution itself. He did this by denouncing a stream of revolutionaries to the authorities as traitors. Remarkably, no one suspected what he was doing!

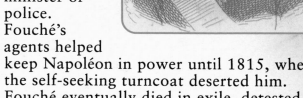

WE SEEK HIM HERE, WE SEEK HIM THERE. The man sought by everyone, English and French alike, was Sir Percy Blakeney, alias the Scarlet Pimpernel (*right*), and hero of the *Scarlet Pimpernel,* written by Baroness Orczy (Montague Barstow) in 1905. Sir Percy leads a band of Englishmen who rescue men and women from the hands of French revolutionaries.

DEATH TO ALL TRAITORS!

Almost all societies have reserved their harshest punishments for traitors. In England, traitors in the upper class were taken by river to the Tower of London (usually via Traitor's Gate, *left*), and beheaded.

Common people were hanged by the neck until half-strangled. Still alive, they were cut down and their bellies sliced open. The intestines were then drawn out and burned. Finally, they were beheaded and their bodies hacked into four quarters. The pieces were displayed on spikes.

In France, punishment was no less gruesome. In 1757, Robert Daumiens was executed in Paris by being torn in quarters by four horses (page 21, *top*) after failing to assassinate King Louis XV.

The Tragedy of Anne Boleyn
Anne Boleyn, the second wife of Henry VIII, was executed on May 19, 1536. Desperate for a male heir, Henry divorced his first wife to marry Anne (left) in 1533. But when she failed to produce a son, he turned to Jane Seymour and had Anne arrested.

Anne was found guilty of treason and sent to the Tower of London, where she was beheaded. Henry married Jane eleven days later.

When is a Traitor not a Traitor?
When Edward I of England tried to conquer Scotland in 1296, Sir William Wallace (below) led Scottish resistance. Eventually he was captured and executed as a traitor in 1305, and his head displayed on London Bridge.

The Scots were horrified. In their eyes, Wallace was not a traitor but a patriot.

Anne Boleyn arrived at Traitor's Gate (below) *in a hysterical state, collapsing at the gate and proclaiming her innocence.*

THE MERCHANT OF PAIN

Horrible as it might sound, torture was considered an art. A skilled torturer (*right*) knew how to cause the maximum pain without his victim passing out or dying, making them talk.

Torture was often used to persuade prisoners to confess their treachery. The threat of torture was often enough to make a victim confess: Limbs were stretched on a rack, or metal boots slowly crushed bones. Those who refused to confess invariably died.

Don't forget that walls have ears!

CARELESS TALK COSTS LIVES

WALLS HAVE EARS

In wartime Britain, posters encouraged citizens to guard against traitors (*left*). Treachery was so feared that many were suspected on the flimsiest of evidence.

During World Wars I and II, life was often uncomfortable for British citizens who happened to have German-sounding names.

In World War II, following Japan's bombing of Pearl Harbor, the United States detained thousands of Japanese fearing they might betray the United States to Japan.

BELLE BOYD'S WAR

In civil wars there are usually no obvious differences between the two sides. This makes spying comparatively easy. Nevertheless, espionage did not play a major part in the Civil War (1861–1865), although it did produce some notable women agents.

Belle Boyd, a teenage Southerner, entered the war when she shot a Northern soldier. Treated leniently by a military court, the "Siren of Shenandoah" became the South's most famous spy. She was arrested six times, imprisoned twice and only the personal intervention of President Lincoln saved her from execution.

Always an extrovert, after the war Belle (*left*) lectured on her exploits, then went on the stage.

THE SCOUTS

During the Civil War both sides relied on skilled riders for information about enemy movements.

After the war, several scouts became famous as heroes of the "Wild West." Perhaps the best known were "Buffalo Bill" Cody (*far left*), and "Calamity Jane" (*left*), who got a job as a scout by pretending to be a man!

TAPPER KERBEY

J.O. Kerbey was a Unionist railroad telegraph operator (the film still, *right*, shows the telegraph system being built). When war broke out, he found work behind Confederate lines. This enabled him to tap into their telegraphs.

Whenever he gathered any useful information, he wrote a letter home, marked with scratches and blots. These were in fact Morse code which referred to key words in the letter. When these words were separated, they made up a hidden message.

WATCH THE BIRDIE!

Lafayette Baker (*far right*), wandered around behind the Confederate lines pretending to take photographs. While snapping Southern soldiers (*right*) with his broken camera, he gathered valuable intelligence, which he passed on to Union leaders in Washington.

Eventually, the lack of finished pictures caused suspicion, and he was arrested. He escaped by filing through the bars of his cell. Back in the North, he was made a Brigadier, in charge of all Unionist intelligence.

THE DETECTIVE SOLDIER

By the mid-1850s, Allan Pinkerton's detective agency was famous throughout the United States. Therefore, when civil war seemed inevitable, the Philadelphia, Wilmington, and Baltimore Railroad Corporation hired Pinkerton to protect it from Confederate saboteurs.

Pinkerton's men soon foiled a Southern attempt to assassinate President Lincoln. Pinkerton (*far left*, with Lincoln, *left*) was asked by the President to organize the North's espionage agency. But his agency was a total failure, and he resigned a year later.

Belle's Escape
Under heavy fire, Belle Boyd (left) *sprinted across open fields to deliver a vital message to Confederate General "Stonewall" Jackson.*

Under Covers?
Confederate sympathizer Rose O'Neal Greenhow (right) *used her charm to seduce Union admirers into handing over useful information.*

THE KING OF SLEUTHHOUNDS

The unification of Germany changed the face of the modern world. Largely the work of Prussian Chancellor Otto von Bismarck (1815-1898), it also owed much to spymaster Wilhelm Stieber (*left*). Stieber learned his craft as a police agent. He joined Bismarck's service in 1863 and was soon the world's most famous spy. First he traveled around Austria disguised as a peddler. The masses of vital information he brought home with him enabled the Prussians to crush the Austrians at Sadova in 1866.

Now in charge of Prussia's secret police, Stieber went to France and returned with three trunkfuls of intelligence. The Franco-Prussian War (1870-1871) followed. Prussia's triumph led directly to the formation of the German Empire.

Stieber died in 1892. Vast crowds came, not to pay their respects but to make sure he was really dead!

Stieber's Dirty Tricks

Stieber's espionage laid the foundation for Prussia's victory at Sadova (main picture).
Disguised as a salesman of pornographic pictures, he collected invaluable military intelligence, bringing Otto von Bismarck's (left) *master plan one step closer to completion.*

CAPTAIN ALFRED DREYFUS

In October 1894 Captain Alfred Dreyfus, a Jewish officer in the French army, was accused of spying. Largely because of his religion, Dreyfus was found guilty and sentenced to life imprisonment.

However, his many supporters did not give up, and he was finally found innocent and released from prison in 1899.

THE ONLY WAY OUT

The man regarded by many as the worst traitor of the 20th century was Austrian spymaster Colonel Alfred Redl.

Homosexual at a time when homosexuality was a crime, in 1913 he was blackmailed by the Russians into handing over information that would cost tens of thousands of Austrian lives in the opening months of World War I. Redl committed suicide (*left*) when his identity was uncovered by his own highly efficient intelligence service.

Being Prepared!
Robert Baden-Powell, founder of the Boy Scout movement (below), was at one time a British spy. His innocent-looking paintings of butterflies in fact contained maps of enemy defenses!

THE VAGABOND SPY. Because they appear innocent and attract little attention, children sometimes make excellent secret agents. Rudyard Kipling (1865–1936) realized this when he wrote his splendid spy novel *Kim*.

Set in India, it tells the story of Kimball O'Hara, an orphan from Lahore. Kim is adopted by his father's old regiment. He becomes a spy and captures vital papers from Russian agents in the Himalaya Mountains.

Test Your Powers of Observation
In the book, a tray of odd items was put in front of Kim for two minutes, then covered up. Kim then had to remember as many items as possible!

ASSASSINATION

The dark shadow of assassination, the ultimate act of traitor and agent, has hung over political leaders since the beginning of history. Among its more notable victims have been Julius Caesar, French President Carnot (*left*), Abraham Lincoln, and British Prime Minister Spencer Perceval. More recently, it has threatened the lives of Pope John Paul II, President Ronald Reagan, and Princess Anne of England.

The word "Assassin" comes from Arabic *hashshash*, meaning "user of hashish (marijuana)." The Assassins were a fanatical 11th-century Muslim sect whose members got high on drugs before setting out on their murderous escapades. In those days assassins used knives or poison. Today, killers can strike from longer range with guns (*main picture*) or explosives.

Buckingham's End
In 1628, George Villiers, England's first Duke of Buckingham was stabbed to death while preparing to attack France (right).

SARAJEVO, 1914
On June 28, 1914, the most momentous assassination of all time took place in Sarajevo, Bosnia. Archduke Franz Ferdinand (*left*), heir to the Austrian throne, was shot dead by Gavrilo Princip, a member of a Serbian-backed nationalist organization.

Austria used the assassination to declare war on Serbia. Serbia's ally Russia, supported by France, entered the conflict. Germany stood by its alliance with Austria. Britain sided with France, and so began World War I.

Death to the Czar!
In 1881 the Russian Czar Alexander II, liberator of the peasants, was blown up by an anarchist bomb (right) *after escaping previous assassination attempts.*

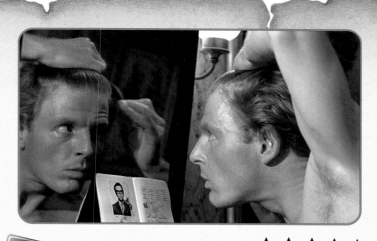

GOLDEN **G**UNS. Filmmakers have fascinated moviegoers with assassins in countless thrillers. From the tongue-in-cheek James Bond film *The Man With the Golden Gun* to the gripping *The Day of the Jackal*, the story of a plot to kill French President Charles de Gaulle, the best assassination films have attracted immense audiences. Edward Fox's superb portrayal of an utterly ruthless, cold-blooded killer (*left*) in *The Day of the Jackal* remains the ultimate assassination masterpiece.

steelwool packing

gases

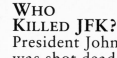

Silencers (above) *work like car exhaust silencers to reduce noise, as steelwool packing slows down the expanding gases in the muzzle. But they also lessen the power of the bullet.*

WHO KILLED JFK?

President John F. Kennedy (*left*) was shot dead in Dallas, Texas, on November 22, 1963. His death is still a mystery.

The accused assassin, Lee Harvey Oswald, was arrested but then killed by a local nightclub operator two days later. Today several conspiracy theories exist: Were the Russians, the Cubans, or the Mafia behind the assassination?

DEATH FOR HIRE

Wherever there is a lot of money, there are people prepared to do whatever is asked of them to earn it. This is the evil world of the hired killer. Such people are no run-of-the-mill gangsters.

Because they plan meticulously, often use disguises, and leave no traces of their deadly work, assassins are rarely brought to justice. In August 1994, one of the most famous assassins, "Carlos the Jackal" (*right*), was arrested only after years of patient investigation.

MATA HARI

During World War I, British intelligence broke several German codes, including that used by the navy, which were of crucial importance. Germany's major espionage triumph was learning about Egland's "Q ships" – merchant ships carrying concealed heavy guns.

Female spies, real and imagined, also came into their own. The best known is Margaretha Geertruida Zelle, known as Mata Hari. Like most other spies, however, she was only concerned with making money. She was executed in October 1917, following her arrest by French authorities.

THE SCHOOL FOR SPIES

During World War I, dark-haired "Tiger Eyes" Elsbeth Schragmuller ran the German spy school in Antwerp. She believed espionage was all a matter of training.

She paid little attention to the personalities of her recruits, most of whom made hopeless agents, while she gained a totally unfounded reputation as a seductive blonde of superhuman ingenuity!

Codename L'Alouette (*"The Lark"*) *Marthe Richer, known as L'Alouette, gathered invaluable intelligence through her affair with a German naval officer in Spain (above).*

FACT AND FICTION. The film *Mata Hari* (1931), starring Greta Garbo, transformed the aging spy of fact into a glamorous female agent (*left*). In World War II, Garbo was a spy herself! Using her contacts in her native Sweden, agent William Stephenson set up escape routes for Allied pilots shot down in Europe.

The Dancing Spy
The Dutch dancer Mata Hari (left), the world's most fictionalized double agent, used her frequent affairs with men to make extra cash by selling their secrets to England and Germany.

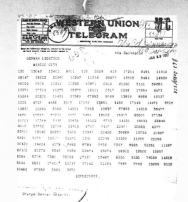

ZIMMERMANN'S TELEGRAM

In January 1917, British intelligence officer Sir Reginald Hall intercepted a telegram from German Secretary of State Arthur Zimmermann to the German ambassador in Mexico City – this changed the course of history. Using a code Hall could decipher, it stated that if the United States joined the war on the Allied side, Germany would back a Mexican invasion of the United States.

Hall leaked the telegram (*left*) to U.S. officials. Incensed, the U.S. government declared war on Germany ten weeks later.

SPOTTERS IN THE AIR

During World War I balloons and aircraft revolutionized information gathering.

Fixed balloons were vulnerable to gunfire. But spotter planes, such as that which noted a crucial gap in the German line during the Battle of the Marne in 1914, quickly reported back all daylight troop movements. At sea, the position of surface fleets, even of individual warships, became almost impossible to hide.

The B.E.5 (left) *was used often by the Allies as a spotter plane.*

Balloons (above left) *were given fins for added stability in the air.*

JAPANESE INTELLIGENCE

The Japanese did not enter the world of international spying until their war with Russia in 1904-1905.

But they were quick to learn – spies in the guise of servants for Russian officers penetrated every part of the garrison at Port Arthur before any attack was made. In 1905, naval intelligence brought a great victory at Tsushima (*left*).

TRAITORS AND HEROES

World War II intelligence operations are marked by countless tales of deception, treachery, and bravery. In 1943 the Allies convinced the Germans they would invade Sardinia, not Sicily, by "planting" a dead civilian as a drowned airman with vital papers in his briefcase. The morale of American servicemen was undermined by broadcasts from Japan of the traitor "Tokyo Rose." But perhaps the most famous story of all is that of beautiful Violette Szabo (*left*).

Szabo became an agent after the death of her French husband. On her second mission she ran into Nazi police. Injured by a fall, she gave covering fire while her French contact escaped (*main picture*). Her life ended in a horrifying tragedy of interrogation and execution.

THE LOVER OF FREEDOM
American-born Amy Elizabeth Thorpe, code-named Cynthia, was Britain's most successful wartime spy. By swapping sex for secrets, she helped get information about the Enigma machine out of Poland (see page 13).

She then used the same tactics to convince the Germans that their French allies were leaking vital intelligence!

Letters and Numbers
The Delastelle code system was used by the British from 1943 onward.

In its simplest form (right), *each letter became a pair of numbers. The word "help," for example, would read 32 41 53 13.*

Further subtleties made the code almost impossible to break.

SAVED BY A TABLE
On July 20, 1944, German army officers tried to assassinate their Führer Adolf Hitler. The bomb left at his headquarters (*left*) killed four people, but not Hitler, who was protected from the blast by a heavy table. The would-be assassins were ruthlessly hunted down and punished by execution.

Hermann Göring, (above) *Hitler's Air Chief, inspects the bomb site the day after the explosion.*

DOCUMENTS IN DOTS

By 1945, technology was playing an ever greater role in intelligence operations.

Sound could be recorded on tape rather than records, and microdot photography allowed a page of writing and diagrams to be reduced to a single dot.

Spies in the field were helped by devices such as compasses hidden in cigarette lighters (right).

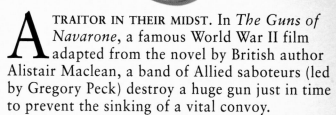

	1	2	3	4	5
1	G	M	P	S	D
2	Q	A	W	C	D
3	N	H	B	T	U
4	E	V	Y	U	R
5	Z	F	L	X	O

A TRAITOR IN THEIR MIDST. In *The Guns of Navarone*, a famous World War II film adapted from the novel by British author Alistair Maclean, a band of Allied saboteurs (led by Gregory Peck) destroy a huge gun just in time to prevent the sinking of a vital convoy.

The commandoes outwit the German military easily enough, but realize only at the last minute that one of their party is a traitor... (*below*).

Fighting to the Last (right)
Lying injured, British agent Violette Szabo covers the escape of a French resistance fighter, firing at the approaching Nazi troops until she runs out of bullets. Szabo, who later died in a concentration camp, was immortalized in the film Carve Her Name With Pride.

THIRTY-NINE STEPS TO FAME

Real-life intelligence work is dangerous, usually dull, and always riddled with deception. Successful spies, generally coldhearted and ruthless, spend most of their time watching and waiting.

However, the imagination of writers and filmmakers can transform this evil, uncertain world into a thrilling fantasy land, where glamorous heroes perform deeds of impossible bravery.

First published in 1915, John Buchan's *The Thirty-Nine Steps* characterizes Richard Hannay as an ordinary man who happens to be in the wrong place at the right time. Before he really knows what's happening, he is suspected of murder, chased over the Scottish Highlands (*main picture*), handcuffed to a beautiful girl, and finds himself trailing a gang of vicious foreign spies.

Often depicted in films (*above left*), the story remains the perfect example of espionage fiction.

"OF ALL THE GIN JOINTS IN ALL THE TOWNS IN ALL THE WORLD, SHE WALKS INTO MINE." The gin joint owner was Rick (Humphrey Bogart). The woman who walked in was Rick's ex-lover Ilse (Ingrid Bergman).

The film was *Casablanca*, the 1942 masterpiece of love and loyalty, set against the backdrop of underground resistance to the Nazis and their henchmen in North Africa. Czech resistance leader Victor Laszlo is trying to flee from Morocco – but will Rick (*above, far left*) betray his identity to Gestapo officer Colonel Strasser (*above, center*)?

ROMANCE OR DRUDGERY? There are two types of spy stories. Following in the vein of the first spy novel, James Fenimore Cooper's *The Spy*, the fantasy school of espionage writing portrays spying as a romantic adventure and spies as either stars or villains. Other espionage writers, typified by John Le Carré, refuse to glamorize. More concerned with fact than fiction, they focus on the sordid and sinister aspects of their subject and the human frailties of their characters.

The spy novel remains as popular as ever (above).

The Man in the Mackintosh
A classic unglamourous spy is Harry Palmer, created by Len Deighton and played by Michael Caine (left).
Palmer is the opposite of James Bond – he hates his job, swears a lot, and is more interested in staying alive than finishing his mission!

SPIES ON SCREEN. Spy stories offer filmmakers everything they need for success – heroes and heroines, evil villains, suspense, and exotic backgrounds. Depending upon the type of film they want, filmmakers simply add their own emphases.

It might be a mystery, as in *The Third Man*, or romance (*The Spy Who Came in from the Cold*), fantasy (*Modesty Blaise*), Cold War brainwashing (*The Manchurian Candidate*), or even comedy (*Casino Royale*).

"The Name's Bond. James Bond"
Thus one of the most popular screen heroes of all time introduces himself – Special Agent 007.
The secret of Bond's success lies with the character British author Ian Fleming created, and Sean Connery's superb first portrayal of the secret agent.
Well-contrived plots, spectacular stunts (right), and glamour are combined to create a series of movies that are irresistible.

ALL THE PRESIDENT'S MEN

"Gentlemen," said U.S. Secretary of State Henry L. Stimson in 1929, "do not read each other's mail." This attitude prevented the United States from setting up a coordinated intelligence service until the Pearl Harbor disaster of December 7, 1941.

During World War II, U.S. intelligence was handled by the Office of Strategic Services (OSS). Abolished in 1945, it was replaced two years later by the Central Intelligence Agency (CIA). During the Cold War era, the CIA grew to become the world's most pervasive and powerful secret service.

Its many successes, such as predicting the Anglo-French invasion of Suez (1956), were balanced by some spectacular failures. These included backing a disastrous Bay of Pigs invasion of Communist Cuba (1961) and failure to warn against Iraq's occupation of Kuwait in 1990.

THE INCREDIBLE OIL SALESMAN

Erick Ericson, perhaps the greatest American spy of World War II, posed as a Swedish oil dealer to collect information on the location of German oil supplies.

He contacted American agents who passed the intelligence to the U.S. Air Force, which promptly blew up the refineries. Though the German secret police tailed him constantly, he managed to avoid capture. The value of cutting German oil supplies was made clear when, during the Battle of the Rhine in 1945, oxen were seen pulling German tanks to the front line.

REDS UNDER THE BED

Information gathering within the United States is shared between the National Security Agency (NSA) which runs communications intelligence, and the Federal Bureau of Investigation (FBI), responsible for counter-espionage. It was founded in 1908 and headed from 1924 to 1972 by J. Edgar Hoover (*left*), now notorious for his enjoyment of dressing up in women's underwear!

At the beginning of the Cold War era, Hoover carried out a campaign against scores of alleged Communists.

Crook at the Top
On June 17, 1972, intruders (below) *were arrested at the Democratic Party's Headquarters in the Watergate Complex. When* it became clear that Republican President Richard Nixon and the CIA were involved, Nixon resigned. The story was immortalized in the film: All the President's Men (right).

MILES OUT?

The weakness of U.S. intelligence was shown when President Franklin D. Roosevelt warned the navy of a Japanese attack on the Philippines, Thailand, or Manila. It came 10 days later, on the U.S. base at Pearl Harbor, in Hawaii (*below*). The disaster forced the United States to enter World War II.

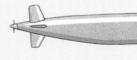

Undercover – and Underwater
In many of the James Bond films there are exciting battles underwater between spies armed with deadly harpoons. One real-life counterpart to the frogsuited agents (below) is the U.S. Navy SEALS unit, formed in 1962 to carry out counterinsurgency operations by Sea, Air, and Land.
Submarines (above) are often used to insert underwater teams, sometimes using the empty torpedo tubes!

ON HER MAJESTY'S SECRET SERVICE

British government intelligence dates from the 16th century (page 14). The modern network was established by 1911. Although often featured in the media, novels, and films, the existence of MI5 was not officially acknowledged until 1989. For many people, the British Secret Service is still most famous for its fictional agent 007 (*left*), and his eccentric bosses "M" and "Q"!

In both World Wars, British intelligence was widely respected. During the era of the Cold War, however, its reputation slumped afeter being infiltrated by Soviet agents.

More recently, sophisticated electronic devices helped intelligence operations combat IRA terrorism in Northern Ireland. One computer searched all telephone calls for key words; others allowed instant access to all known information on suspects.

MI6's FALKLANDS FLOP

On April 2, 1982 Argentinean forces (*above*) swiftly overran the Falkland Islands, a British colony in the South Atlantic off the coast of Argentina. Prime Minister Margaret Thatcher dispatched a large task force. Two months later, the islands were back in British hands.

But why had the invasion not been foreseen? Following a report, MI6 was forced to re-organize and bring itself up-to-date.

MI5 SPYHUNTER STELLA

In 1991, England announced the appointment of Stella Rimmington (*left*) as the new director general of counterintelligence.

This was the first time such an appointment had been made public and the first time a woman had headed a Western intelligence agency.

Since the end of the Cold War era, MI5 (Military Intelligence Department 5), has taken over anti-terrorist activities from the English police, for example combatting the IRA in Northern Ireland.

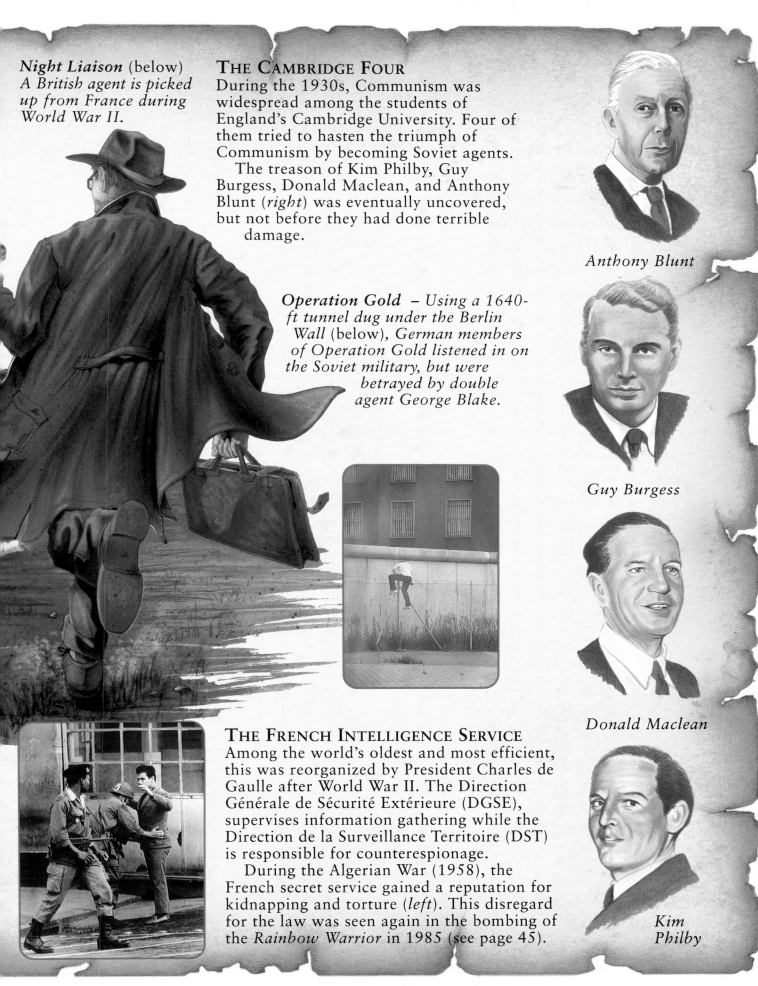

Night Liaison (below)
A British agent is picked up from France during World War II.

THE CAMBRIDGE FOUR

During the 1930s, Communism was widespread among the students of England's Cambridge University. Four of them tried to hasten the triumph of Communism by becoming Soviet agents.

The treason of Kim Philby, Guy Burgess, Donald Maclean, and Anthony Blunt (*right*) was eventually uncovered, but not before they had done terrible damage.

Operation Gold – *Using a 1640-ft tunnel dug under the Berlin Wall* (below), *German members of Operation Gold listened in on the Soviet military, but were betrayed by double agent George Blake.*

THE FRENCH INTELLIGENCE SERVICE

Among the world's oldest and most efficient, this was reorganized by President Charles de Gaulle after World War II. The Direction Générale de Sécurité Extérieure (DGSE), supervises information gathering while the Direction de la Surveillance Territoire (DST) is responsible for counterespionage.

During the Algerian War (1958), the French secret service gained a reputation for kidnapping and torture (*left*). This disregard for the law was seen again in the bombing of the *Rainbow Warrior* in 1985 (see page 45).

Anthony Blunt

Guy Burgess

Donald Maclean

Kim Philby

BEHIND THE IRON CURTAIN

During the Cold War era, the Soviet intelligence system – known as the KGB – was a massive organization. It employed 350,000 officers and had units covering every angle of intelligence operations, from data gathering and industrial espionage to assassination.

Between 1954 and 1990, the KGB (its badge is *left*) scored numerous intelligence coups. It even managed to bug the bedroom of England's Queen Elizabeth II and Prince Philip!

Of greater value to the Russians was the sensitive information American GI Robert Lee Johnson plundered from the Armed Forces Courier Centre in Paris. The FBI uncovered Johnson's treachery in 1964 and he was given a 25-year jail sentence. Eight years later, he was stabbed to death by his son, a Vietnam veteran.

DEAD-LETTER BOXES

Unless a meeting is necessary, agents often prefer to use Dead-Letter Boxes (DLBs). These are special places were messages can be left for another agent to pick up.

During the 1980s, the KGB used a DLB in a marble column in a London church, the Brompton Oratory (*above*). A simple blue mark on a lamppost outside the church told an agent that a message was waiting for him inside. A chalk mark on a nearby bench indicated that the first mark had been seen.

Gorky Park
Few Cold War spy stories captured the bleak underworld of KGB espionage better than the 1980s thriller Gorky Park, *starring William Hurt and Lee Marvin* (below right).

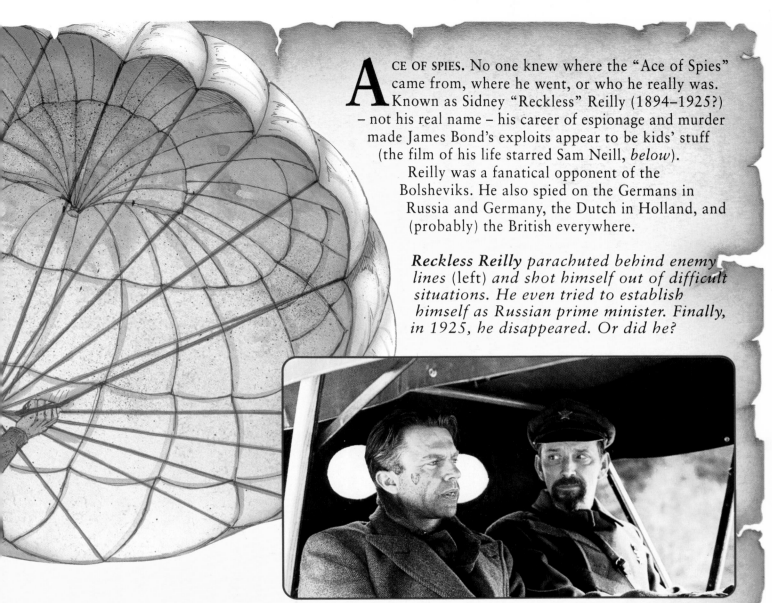

ACE OF SPIES.

No one knew where the "Ace of Spies" came from, where he went, or who he really was. Known as Sidney "Reckless" Reilly (1894–1925?) – not his real name – his career of espionage and murder made James Bond's exploits appear to be kids' stuff (the film of his life starred Sam Neill, *below*).

Reilly was a fanatical opponent of the Bolsheviks. He also spied on the Germans in Russia and Germany, the Dutch in Holland, and (probably) the British everywhere.

Reckless Reilly parachuted behind enemy lines (left) and shot himself out of difficult situations. He even tried to establish himself as Russian prime minister. Finally, in 1925, he disappeared. Or did he?

A SOVIET DOUBLE AGENT

In April 1994, the former CIA chief of Soviet counterintelligence Aldrich Ames was caught after nine years of spying for the Soviet Union.

He began his career as a double agent in April 1985, when he had arranged to meet with the former Soviet embassy diplomat, Sergei Chuvakin "to discuss broad foreign policy issues" – a scheme allowing him to reach the KGB without arousing suspicion.

Ames then used Chuvakin to pass a secret message on to the KGB, which contained the names of ten Soviet double agents who had offered to work for the CIA. Ames' scheme eventually earned him an estimated $1.5 million.

Kalugin reveals all
Few KGB agents enjoyed a more spectacular career than Oleg Kalugin (left). In 1958, he came to the United States as an exchange student and began recruiting spies for the KGB.

Later, as head of the Russian foreign counter-intelligence, he had contact with several British double agents and helped in assassinations.

Finally, he broke with the Communists and told all he knew in his best-selling book Spymaster.

THE ART OF SPYING

"Reckless Reilly" (page 39) was a brilliant spy, Mata Hari (page 28) was a poor one. The key differences between them were discretion, ruthlessness, and brains. Reilly was a multilingual, crafty, and determined professional, prepared to kill to get what he wanted. Mata Hari was an amateur, who failed to keep her activities secret and could not distinguish valuable intelligence from useless rumor.

"Tiger Eyes" Schragmuller was wrong in believing spies can be made by training alone. Modern intelligence agencies carefully screen all candidates before employing them. A sound personality is essential. Heavy drinkers, gamblers, and philanderers can be blackmailed. The unintelligent and inefficient are liabilities, too.

Gadgets Galore!
No Bond film is complete without the latest gadgets: here 007 tries out an autogyro in You Only Live Twice *(below).*

A Successful Plant
For the modern spy, instruction in practical matters, such as safe-breaking, photography (above left), dead-letter boxes and even assassination, is quickly done. Planting an agent in a sensitive position takes far longer. (It took the Russians ten years to get Johnson (page 37) into a position where he had access to really sensitive information.)

TOOLS OF THE TRADE
Although the microchip has enabled spy equipment to become smaller, the basic tools of the trade have remained unchanged for decades. They have five basic functions: (A) recording sound, pictures, and words; (B) transmitting messages; (C) assassination and self-defense; (D) observation; (E) concealment. These require many of the types of devices shown below, as well as hair dye and wigs.

Seven Deadly Devices
1 Mini micro-film container in talc container
2 Letterbomb spray
3 Mini cigarette box recorder
4 Mini binoculars
5 Cufflink box transmitter
6 Mini camera
7 Mobile phone

THE CLASSIC FICTIONAL SPY dresses in a long coat, carries an attaché case and wears dark glasses! But what do spies look like in the 1990s? The answer is – probably just like everyone else! Look at this picture *(right)* – can you guess which one is the spy?

BACK ON THE GROUND

During the 1980s, intelligence networks placed more emphasis on technology (e.g., spy satellites, page 45) than agents in the field. But Iraq's surprise invasion of Kuwait in 1990 showed the weakness of this practice.

Since then, the CIA has recruited more agents in the troubled areas of the world. Spies help ascertain for example, whether a factory is producing fertilizer or chemical weapons.

Not What It Seems

Ready for anything, this Cold War spy (left) has mirrored glasses, a compass wristwatch, a camera lighter, a shooting cigarette case, bugs in his tie, belt, suspenders, and deadly gas-firing pens.

No real agent would ever carry all these gadgets at the same time!

AN UNUSUAL WEAPON

In September 1978, the Bulgarian writer Georgi Markov was assassinated with a poisoned umbrella that fired tiny pellets of deadly poison.

At the time, Markov felt just a jab in his thigh. But three days later, he was dead!

Trigger and safety spring

Mini gas cylinder

Micro poison pellet

Micro-bore barrel

RED ALERT, CUBA!

In 1962, the Cold War was at its peak. U-2 spy planes spotted Soviet nuclear missile sites on Cuba, within easy range of the United States. President John F. Kennedy demanded destruction of the site. President Nikita Khrushchev refused, unless the United States dismantled bases in Turkey. Kennedy held firm.

Missile-laden ships near Cuba and the nuclear arsenals on red alert, contributed to two days of unbearable tension. Khruschev backed down and the Soviet ships turned back. The Cuban sites were destroyed and nuclear war was averted.

The Cold War initiated a spree of espionage. From 1946-1990 the CIA and KGB monitored each other's progress in the multi-billion dollar arms race, watched for unusual military maneuvers, and tried to win allies in other parts of the world.

Victims or traitors? On June 19, 1953 Ethel and Julius Rosenberg (left) were executed in the electric chair for spying for the USSR. Both denied the charges, and to this day their guilt is uncertain.

BOMBS FOR ALL

During World War II, the United States refused to share its atomic bomb secrets with its Soviet ally. So the U.S.S.R. had to get them by other means. Alan Nunn and Klaus Fuchs, physicists with Communist views, were only too pleased to oblige. When caught, both claimed that knowledge was international property!

LYING IN SIN

In March 1963, Minister Jack Profumo lied to parliament about his affair with prostitute Christine Keeler. When it was revealed that a Soviet spy shared her favors, Profumo's career was finished.

*It's a Scandal
The film Scandal (left) retold the story of Christine Keeler and her affairs with British Minister Jack Profumo and Russian agent, Eugene Ivanov.*

THE SPY PLANE

Early spy planes were converted fighters or bombers. The first spy plane, the Lockheed U-2, flew in 1955. Very light and with a massive wingspan, it could reach 100,000 ft. It was superseded by SR-71, able to cross the Atlantic in under two hours.

Today there is much speculation about the *Aurora* (*above left*), a mystery reconnaissance plane said to fly for thousands of miles without refuelling.

The Lockheed SR-71
Known as the Blackbird, the sleek SR-71 (left) was the ultimate spy plane of the 1960s.

Surveillance

Surveillance is a high altitude record of an area up to 300 miles in diameter.

Imaging is photography of specific areas or objects.

Imaging

Sideways Looking Airborne Radar (SLAR) records on photographic film a broad strip of terrain along the aircraft's flight path.

SLAR

MISSILE

Tell-Tale Signs
Reading aerial spy photographs (above) is a skilled art. Tell-tale signs of something suspicious are roads and railways that go nowhere, and dead camouflage foliage in the spring or summer.

SPY SWAP
On May 1, 1960 a U-2 spy aircraft was shot down over the Soviet Union. Piloted by CIA agent Gary Powers (*above*), the incident greatly embarrassed the United States. In 1962 Powers was released in exchange for Rudolf Abel, a KGB colonel caught spying in the United States.

COOPERATION AND COMPETITION

With the collapse of the Communist bloc in Eastern Europe, the Cold War era came to an end. But spying continued. Attention was turned to the Middle East by Sadam Hussein's invasion of Kuwait. Then came conflicts in the former Soviet republics, and Yugoslavia, Somalia, and Rwanda. Wherever there was war, accurate intelligence was required.

Intelligence technology progressed rapidly, spies became computer literate, and agencies employed highly skilled hackers. Some governments, such as the French and Chinese, allowed their agencies to conduct industrial espionage. The fight against international terrorism brought greater co-operation. Even so, England and the United States found it hard to agree on who was responsible for bringing down Pan Am Flight 103 over Scotland.

Modern Technology, such as closed-circuit TV (above) can make life difficult for spies, but gadgets like a hand-held satellite phone (right) could help an agent to avoid being bugged.

INDUSTRIAL ESPIONAGE

Since the Industrial Revolution, espionage has moved into the commercial sphere. Large companies regularly employ agents to discover what their competitors are doing.

Phone tapping, bugging, and computer hacking are commonplace. Detection is rare, but in 1993 French officials disclosed a 21-page government document that targeted 21 American aerospace companies for industrial espionage.

THE SPY IN THE SKY

As soon as the U.S.S.R. launched the first satellite, *Sputnik I* (1957), intelligence services heralded the arrival of a wonderful new piece of espionage equipment (*center*).

Within a decade, the Soviets had launched nuclear-powered *Cosmos* spy satellites. At first, spy satellites were able to send back pictures of objects the size of an airfield. Then they could pick out single aircraft.

By the 1990s, satellites such as the U.S. *KH-12* were supposedly powerful enough to identify details on an individual person. Is Big Brother watching YOU?

Global Warning – Today's spy satellites are used to monitor hot spots across the world, such as Serbian positions in Bosnia (above).

THE FIRM. Adapted from John Grisham's novel, the movie *The Firm* tells the story of a young lawyer (Tom Cruise) who joins a law firm that is a front for a Mafia money-laundering operation (*right*).

The size of criminal organizations like the Mafia and the growth of the drug trade has forced agencies like the FBI to spend an increasing amount of time combatting them.

THE SINKING OF THE RAINBOW WARRIOR

In 1985, two French secret service agents blew up the Greenpeace ship *Rainbow Warrior* in Auckland Harbor, New Zealand (*left*). The vessel was there to monitor French nuclear tests. Though the two spies were arrested, heavy-handed French diplomacy soon ensured their safe return home.

Human rights, animal rights, and environmental groups are increasingly a target for governments who want embarrassing secrets to remain hidden from the public eye. And with the Cold War at an end, there are more than enough spies to go around...

TODAY'S WORLD OF SPYING

The map below shows from where today's main espionage agencies operate. The greatest change in recent years has been the break-up of the KGB into separate agencies in each of the former republics of the Soviet Union.

(1) CIA/FBI, United States
See pages 34-35 and 42-43.

(2) DGSE, France
See pages 37 and 45.

(3) BND (Federal Intelligence Agency), Germany
Formed in 1956, its efforts to infiltrate the old USSR met with disaster.

(4) MI5/MI6, United Kingdom
See pages 36 and 42.

(5) FIS, Russia
See pages 38-39 and 42-43.

(6) DS (Darjavna Sugurmost), Bulgaria
The old Communist service had close links with the KGB. It assassinated Georgi Markov.

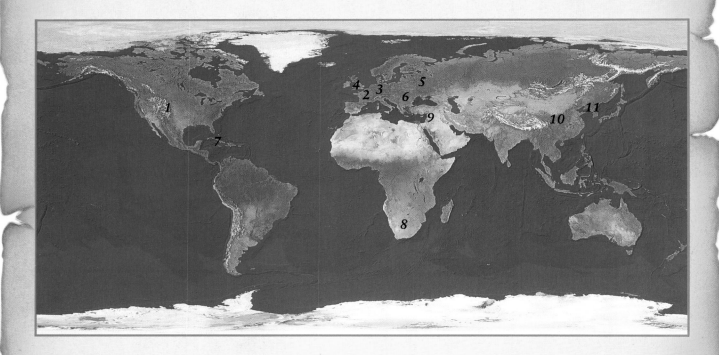

(7) DGI (Direccion General de Inteligencia) Cuba
Formed by Castro, and until recently controlled by the KGB. In the past the DGI trained terrorists from organizations such as the IRA. In recent years it has focused more on countering internal threats to Castro's rule.

(8) NIS (National Intelligence Service), South Africa
Created in 1979 to replace BOSS, which had gained a reputation for ruthlessness and a total disregard for international law and human rights.

(9) Mossad (Israeli Institution for Intelligence and Special Services)
Regarded by many as the finest secret service in the world, it proved its ability in the Six Day War against Egypt in 1972.

(10) CELD (Central External Liaison Department), China
CELD provides a global intelligence service while the Cheng pao k'o (Political Security Section) monitors internal affairs within China.

(11) KISS (South Korean Intelligence and Security Service)
Despite its name, KISS is a tough, ruthless agency devoted mostly to the ongoing battle against North Korea.

SPIES AND TRAITORS' TIMELINE

1370 B.C. Mursilis sends his chamberlain to spy on Egyptian queen Anches-en-amun.

1200 B.C. Rahab helps the two spies of Joshua escape from Jericho.

356-323 B.C. Rule of Alexander the Great who used the scroll and staff cipher (*below*).

218 B.C. Hannibal sends spies to Gaul to plan his route over the Alps into Italy.

44 B.C. Julius Caesar stabbed to death in the Roman Senate.

11th century A.D. Rise of the troubadours – roving singers who also acted as spies.

1095 First Crusade, when Normans (*below*) used pigeons to send secret messages.

1206-1223 Genghis Khan sets up the *yam*, his courier and spy system.

1306 Kildrummy falls to English Prince Edward after Osbourne the blacksmith betrays the castle.

1536 Anne Boleyn is beheaded by Henry VIII, despite her innocence.

1587 Elizabeth I orders the execution of Mary Queen of Scots after her spymaster Walsingham uncovers various Catholic plots to assassinate Elizabeth.

November 5, 1605 Day that Guy Fawkes planned to blow up James I and his parliament.

1624-1642 Cardinal Richelieu creates the "Black Cabinet," his French spy network.

1633 *Oprichnina* formed by Ivan the Terrible.

1660-1669 Samuel Pepys writes his diary in a secret shorthand.

1728-1810 Life of the French spy Chevalier D'Eon, alias "Madame de Beaumont" (*left*).

1776 American Nathan Hale is hanged by the British as a spy. Benjamin Franklin helps Britain to spy on America.

1799-1815 Fouché terrorizes France as head of Napoléon's secret police force.

1840 Samuel Morse is granted a patent for the electric telegraph and his famous code.

1861-1865 American Civil War between North and South, during which Belle Boyd (*top*) and Rose O'Neal Greenhow spied for the Confederates, and Alan Pinkerton and J.O. Kerbey worked for the Unionists.

1866 Prussian spymaster Wilhelm Stieber spies in Austria disguised as a peddler.

1894 French Jew Alfred Dreyfus is falsely accused of being a traitor.

1914-1918 World War I spies Mata Hari and Marthe Richer use their feminine charms to gain important intelligence.

1915 Russian sailors pick up the body of a dead German naval officer, and discover the secret German navy codes.

1939 Violette Szabo helps the Allies to get plans of the German Enigma machine.

1944 German army officers fail in their attempt to assassinate Hitler.

1950s FBI leader J.Edgar Hoover hunts down suspected Communists in the United States.

1960 Gary Powers is shot down over the Soviet Union.

1962 Cuban missile crisis almost starts a world war.

1973 President Nixon is forced to resign after intruders are discovered in the Watergate Complex.

April 1994 Aldrich Ames is caught spying for the Soviet Union.

INDEX

Photo credits *Abbreviations: t – top, m – middle, b – bottom, l – left, r – right.*
Cover: EON/MGM Ltd (Courtesy Kobal Collection); 4-5: Lowndes Prods. (Courtesy Kobal); 6b:
Commonwealth/SIP (Courtesy Kobal); 11t, 22b, 33m: Paramount (Courtesy Kobal); 11b: Cannon
(Courtesy Kobal); 17b: Rank (Courtesy Kobal); 27t: Universal (Courtesy Kobal); 31: Columbia (Courtesy
Kobal); 33b: MGM/UA (Courtesy Kobal); 35t: Warner Bros. (Courtesy Kobal); 36t United Artists
(Courtesy Kobal); 39t: Kobal Collection; 6-7, 9b, 11m, 13l, 14t & b, 16b, 17t, 18 both, 19 both, 21t,
25t, 26t & b, 29, 33tl & tr: Mary Evans Picture Library; 7, 8b, 9t, 10, 20m & b, 21b, 23t & m, 24, 25m,
26m, 30 both, 35b, 37b, 42t: Hulton Deutsch Collection; 8t, 14m: Stewart Ross; 13r: Imperial War
Museum; 16t, 27m & b, 28, 32b, 36b, 37t, 38b, 39b, 40 both, 42b, 43, 44b, 45t & m: Frank Spooner
Pictures; 20t, 25b, 34, 38t, 41, 44m: Roger Vlitos; 23b: Library of Congress, Washington DC; 44-45:
NASA; 45b: Greenpeace Picture Library; 46: Science Photo Library.